ANTHONY TAYLOR

Mental Toughness Metaphors

Stories to Inspire Resilience for Parents, Coaches, Trainers , Teachers and Thinkers

To Jo, Beth, Jess, Will & Merryn
&
Ed (the dog) you challenge my mental toughness every day!
xxx

And in memory of

Alison Caldwell
One of the kindest and mentally strong people I ever met.

For Paul, Harriet & Spencer

Contents

Foreword

The Mental Toughness concept has emerged as one of the most important concepts in the field of people and organisation development. It brings another dimension and another perspective to our understanding of personality.

It draws out what psychologist call "individual differences". We are all very individual – we all respond to events in our own way - and the whole area of personality is nuanced.

If we are to stop thinking in terms of "types" we need to understand those nuances and, most importantly, be able to describe these to others so that they can grasp their significance.

That means describing the concepts and the constructs in different ways.

Anthony has usefully chosen to adopt the use of metaphors to a useful and valuable source of that insight. Metaphors can simplify what is complex and personality is complex. The use of metaphors provokes reflection and thinking about the meaning of the metaphor as well as illustrating what the concept can mean.

To use a metaphor "this book helps to shine a light on who we are".

Doug Strycharczyk
CEO, AQR International,
Author of Developing Mental Toughness; Developing Resilient

Organisations;
Developing Mental Toughness in Young People

Preface

Growing up I remember my Mum reading many Aesop's fables to me. To this day I can still conjure a mental image of my Mum reading them to me and the happiness I felt.

Stories have that power, not only in themselves but in the situations in which they are told. Stories are how we human beings have communicated for thousands of years. Long before the internet and even before written language we communicated through pictures and stories.

Powerful stories don't have to be long in themselves. Often shorter is better. Dr Seuss is a master at that.

I'm no Dr Seuss but what I have done is provide a collection of short stories and metaphors to help you begin to think about and understand mental toughness. In 2020, the year many of us will never forget as long as we live, due to the start of the global pandemic, mental toughness was a quality that was much needed.

Yet it's often misunderstood and misinterpreted. I hope this book will begin to change that and to help each of us think about our own mental toughness and how we can begin to make better use of this 'plastic personality trait'.

This book is as much for adults as children, and if you are a parent, I hope you will enjoy reading these stories to your children and that they provide you both with many happy memories, like Aesop's fables did for me.

Acknowledgement

Credit must firstly go to my parents for instilling in me a clear set of values and morals and for teaching me, through their actions and beliefs, about mental toughness. They embody what it means to be mentally tough and to do it with high levels of emotional intelligence.

I'd also like to acknowledge the work of Doug Strycharczyck, Peter Clough, Jim Loehr, and every other researcher and practitioner in the field of mental toughness. Without their work, we would not have such a valuable tool with which to work with people to help them achieve their goals and dreams.

I'd also like to thank Nick Owen, author of three outstanding books on stories and metaphors, see references section, all are available on Amazon. It was these two titles that stirred my imagination and gave me the idea for this book. Nick's words of encouragement in several emails also helped. I would urge anyone to get a copy of his books. The learning in their pages is invaluable.

Praise for Mental Toughness Metaphors

"Anthony has brought together the key aspects of mental toughness in a beautifully crafted set of stories and metaphors. Anyone interested in developing their own mental toughness will undoubtedly feel inspired by the stories. A lovely, easy to read book - highly recommended!"

- Penny Mallory, motivational speaker, former rally champion and TV presenter

In "Mental Toughness Metaphors" Anthony Taylor clearly and concisely explains what Mental Toughness is and why it's important. He then uses 20 engaging metaphors to bring the subject to life and make the theoretical truly actionable. A thoroughly enjoyable and very helpful read that I'll be coming back to time and again.

- Matt Wilkinson, Marketing Strategist and Visiting Fellow at Cranfield School of Management

"Mental Toughness Metaphors is an entertaining and easily readable publication, either in one go or referenced chapter by chapter. Mental Toughness expert Anthony Taylor has expertly distilled some of the complexity of the subject with some insightful observations and questions surrounding some original and new stories that will appeal to children and adults alike. A must-read."

- Paul Lyons, Australian Mental Toughness practitioner

"Anthony shares his expertise and passion for mental toughness in an engaging and approachable format that inspires anyone, of any age, to develop what is undoubtedly one of the most important life skills of our current times. The metaphors and questions posed offer a refreshing perspective, avoiding the typical textbook overwhelm, helping us understand and apply these mental toughness tips within our daily lives. A must-read for anyone wanting to thrive on the challenges of life!"

- Alex Staniforth, Record-breaking Adventurer, Endurance Athlete, Resilience Speaker and Author

"I highly recommend this little gem of a book for anyone who wants to develop more self-awareness and mental toughness. It's filled with some great stories and insights told in a simple, powerful and easily digestible way!"

- Natalia Cohen, Record-breaking ocean rower and Inspirational Speaker

"Anthony has curated a wonderful selection of short stories and fables, which not only have the ability to put a smile on your face and warm your heart – but with his wise counsel and consideration he is able to contextualise and make relevant to help challenge our own perceptions and mindset."

- Craig Hamer, Consultant, Executive Coach & Mental Toughness Master Practitioner

"Margaret Atwood said, 'You're never going to kill storytelling because it's built into the human plan.' Whether fact or fiction, there is so much to glean from stories to aid us on our journey through life. Anthony has pulled together a fabulous collection of short stories that speak of hope, encouragement and triumph over adversity. Such stories are invaluable for all ages. Soak them up, share them with friends and family and extract the beautiful truths that will ease your burden and broaden your shoulders. This is a great resource!"

   - Paul Nixon, Learning & Development Specialist, Vodafone

"By bringing together such a group of readable, engaging and relevant stories, Anthony has created a book that people of all ages can use in all aspects of their lives to help with their mental toughness. It is the sort of book that will be read and re-read many times to help them cope with what their life journey throws at them. I would recommend that all teenagers read this book before they enter adulthood."

   - Jonty Warneken, Disabled Ice Swimmer, Director - International Ice Swimming Association

"I love this book, really easy reading and digestible. Quick, short and to the point stories that really resonate and make you think about how you approach things to maintain a positive mindset and outlook."

   - Dave Birchall, Head of People & Performance, Node4 Ltd

"Anthony provides an opportunity for a simple and clear understanding of mental toughness and how important it is for us to succeed with our daily challenges. Through a collection of short stories and metaphors, he is able to transport you to a new level of thinking about how you can enhance your

ix

understanding and begin to think about mental toughness. Anthony uses his own reflections to enhance your introspective thinking so as to implement the strategies he uncovers. I will be using many of his wonderful stories in my own coaching from now on."

- Michelle Bakjac, Psychologist, ICF Credentialed Coach and Trainer, Bakjac Consulting, Adelaide, South Australia

"Mental Toughness Metaphors is a great read! I can relate to everything stated in this book - it really does make you stop and reflect on your own life experiences! As a teacher, I feel that these are such important messages that we need to share and teach our children to help prepare them for life and the challenges they will face."

- Steve Hill MBE, Teacher, Adventurer, Author, Extreme Ultra Marathon Runner, Charity Fundraiser, Ambassador for DofE Award, Motivational Speaker

1

What is Mental Toughness?

Mental toughness is one of those terms that means different things to different people. It can be quite a polarising term, conjuring up images of male machismo. Of bulging biceps and 'balls', the unfortunate metaphor for courage, a never-say-die attitude and in some cases, downright stupidity. It's also sometimes mistaken for a lack of compassion and empathy.

Jim Loehr, a leading sports psychologist in the 1980s and founder of the Johnson & Johnson Human Performance Institute, popularised the use of the term 'Mental Toughness'.

He defined it as:

"The ability to consistently perform towards the upper range of your capabilities, regardless of competitive circumstances."

Since then, world leaders in the field, Professor Peter Clough and Doug Strycharczyck, have built on the work of Loehr and others like Kobasa and Diensteber to develop the 4Cs model of mental toughness.

They define it as:

"A plastic *personality trait* which determines, *in some part,* how individuals respond mentally when exposed to stressors, pressure and challenge... *irrespective of the prevailing situation."*

What is the 4Cs model?

Most personality models and measures assess the behavioural aspects of personality (how we act). Mental toughness differs in that it assesses something more fundamental – "how we think". In other words, why we act and respond to events. It enables us to understand mindset in a very practical way.

Research carried out under the direction of Professor Peter Clough in 2002, then of Huddersfield University, identified the four key components (constructs) of mental toughness. These are called the 4Cs. In 2017, work by Doug Strycharczyk, Dr John Perry, and Professor Clough, allowed the concept to be expanded to eight factors to be understood and assessed around the 4Cs.

This 4Cs model is shown below:

Each section, or slice, can be explained as follows:

CONTROL

Life Control – I really believe in myself, I can do it

Emotional Control – I can manage my emotions and the emotions of others

COMMITMENT

Goal Orientation – I set goals and like the idea of working toward goals

Achievement Orientation – I do what it takes to keep promises and achieve goals

CHALLENGE

Risk Orientation – I stretch myself, welcoming new and different experiences

Learning Orientation – I learn from what happens, including setbacks

CONFIDENCE

In Abilities – I believe I have the ability to do it, or can acquire the ability

Interpersonal Confidence – I can influence others as much as they do me

It is consistent with motivational models such as Maslow's Hierarchy of Needs and with all leadership models providing an additional level of understanding to support development in these areas.

It is also relevant for all soft skills development such as team building, interpersonal skills, communication skills, emotional intelligence, etc. It has a particularly strong role in coaching and mentoring where it supports the development of a client's self-awareness of their strengths and their development needs...

and why these exist. It is also widely used in talent management programmes to support the transition to new and challenging roles.

Usefully, the mental toughness concept embraces a number of similar ideas such as mindset, grit, character, resilience and learned optimism in one comprehensive framework.

Is mental toughness important?

There are many reasons why mental toughness is important. In fact, with over 7 billion people on the planet, I'd suggest each one would have a multitude of reasons why mental toughness would be important to them.

However, to make it just a little more digestible, let's break it down into some key areas. Published research and case studies from around the world show that mental toughness is a major factor in several key areas.

Performance

The first and perhaps most obvious one is performance. Plenty of studies show that it explains up to 25 percent of the variation in performance between individuals. Whether that is at work, in education or at play, the higher a person's mental toughness the better they perform under stress, pressure and challenge.

Mental Agility

At work, it translates into mental agility. People are more likely to do more and often to a higher standard. They are committed and resilient, meaning that despite setbacks they still achieve what they set out to. They seek to learn from failures rather than running away from them. They thrive on pressure and rise to the challenge. It shows up in their behaviours too. Who do you know who is more engaged, more positive, demonstrates more of a 'can-do' attitude than others? Do they deal well with change, embracing it and moving through the change curve quickly?

Wellbeing

The wellbeing agenda for businesses has never been so important. Not only is sickness absence costings businesses £millions every year there are now legal obligations to looking after the mental health of your employees.

What the research shows us is that those with higher levels of mental toughness have higher levels of wellbeing. Research by Huddersfield University in 2020, looked at the relationship between mental toughness, job loss and mental health issues during the COVID-19 pandemic. They found that mentally tough individuals appeared to report lower levels of depression, anxiety, and stress.

Mentally tough people tend to show more contentment and are better at stress management. It's not that they can take more stress than others, it's that they often manage themselves better and take the steps to ensure the stress they face doesn't become overwhelming.

Their mindset in this area is a big help too. They see stress, pressure, and challenge differently which reduces the negative effects. They are also less prone to bullying both in terms of engaging in bullying behaviours and feeling like they are being bullied. As they are typically confident in their abilities and interpersonal skills they are willing to stand their ground and share their opinion. They don't see opposite opinions as a threat to their abilities.

Aspirations

It's easy to spot the more mentally strong when it comes to aspirations. They have a thirst to challenge and stretch themselves. They are happier outside of their comfort zone than someone more mentally sensitive and will often seek new challenges.

Failure is seen as temporary and a lesson, rather than permanent and a reflection on their abilities. In today's world of fast-paced change, cloaked by uncertainty and ambiguity, teams with members displaying this trait will be the ones that perform.

It is also a major factor in retention, as mentally tough people stick to the task in hand and ride out the storms along the way. When blended with emotional intelligence the mentally tough person has the edge.

In the world of work, it is key for leadership and staff development, particularly within change and talent management programmes.

A Word of caution

A high level of mental toughness can have an upside or a downside but that depends on self-awareness.

There are many benefits to understanding mental toughness both at an individual and team level. I hope the rest of this book sparks your interest in learning more about the subject and yourselves.

2

The Three Steps to Success

Former Grand Slam Champ and world number one tennis player, Boris Becker was being interviewed on the radio one day.

"Have you always been better than everyone else", asked the interviewer?

"No," he replied. When he was young, he had been identified as a prospect, although other lads his age were better and some more naturally talented. He added that sometimes he had to play the best girls because the boys were too good for him.

"So what happened to those boys," asked the interviewer, "how did you go on to gain so much success and they didn't?"

"Well, they just didn't make it. Even with their natural talent, they didn't have what it takes, because it takes much more than that," he replied.

"So what does it take then?", asked the interviewer.

"You've got to want it badly enough."

"So, that's the secret? Wanting it badly enough?"

"No, not just that. It takes discipline. No matter how much God-given talent, you must have the discipline to nurture and develop what talent you have. You've got to decide what's most important to you and give up many other things so you can focus on that."

"So, that's the secret, then, discipline?"

"No, not entirely. There's another and this is harder than the first two. It's humility. You need humility, no matter how good you think you are. You need humility to listen to your coaches, to take their advice, to test and try new things and to admit you don't know everything. To accept that maybe you aren't quite as good as you think you are or would like to be just yet."

"These are the three secrets to my success," said Becker.

. . .

Primary Source: Nick Owen

Mental Toughness Factors: Challenge, Commitment

My takeaways:

1. Talent will only get you so far. Commitment and mindset are often more important.
2. No person is an island. No matter how good you are, you'll need the support of other people to achieve your potential.

Questions to consider:

1. Do you have all three?
2. Which one would you say you need to improve on?
3. If you improved that by just 10%, what difference would that make?

3

The Grass Parable

As I walked the hills behind my house this past Christmas Eve, I noticed a clump of new-green grass cracking the soil where it broke through.

Not more than half an inch high, but nonetheless, I stopped and marvelled. You see, just a few days before, the temperature plummeted to 10 degrees Fahrenheit, hardly the weather you'd expect to see grass sprouting.

After I soaked in the beauty of green against a dormant, desert-scape, I mourned for the short life expectancy of this grass. Very soon, possibly tonight, it would wither from the frost and all its efforts pushing through the hard Nevada ground would have been in vain. Two days later, though, it continued to grow.

The following morning, it had been mowed down to half its size, a rare winter treat for a quail or cottontail.

The weather turned, as is expected in the Great Basin Desert.

I checked the thermometer for the overnight low: 2 degrees. The daytime high barely reached 20 degrees. I knew my grass was gone.

Why would I care about a little mound of green on a walking path? After some thought, I realised we are like this grass. We make substantial breakthroughs only to fall back.

This grass's attempt wasn't wasted.

It probably wasn't dead; it was only dormant. Its roots didn't appear overnight, just because the sprigs did. It grew because it had a good foundation. In its short time, it took advantage of the sun, storing energy for its survival. In the meantime, it gave sustenance to the wildlife around it, making them stronger.

We rise. We lose ground. But we must endure. Life is not always on an upward trend. Think of the grass. Build your roots—your core truths—so that when adversity hits, you can break out into the sunshine.

. . .

Source: Kathleen Berry

Mental Toughness: Commitment

My takeaways:

1. Setbacks are inevitable, what matters is that we keep getting back up.

2. Our roots rely on many things: other people, self-esteem, clear goals and awareness of our values and the reason why we are striving to achieve something

Questions to consider:

1. How do cope with setbacks? Do you see them as temporary and external to you or permanent and internal?
2. How could you think like a mentally tough person about a recent event that caused you some stress or upset?
3. Are you clear on your values and purpose?

4

The Chinese Farmer

A Chinese farmer used an old horse to till his fields.

One day, the horse escaped into the hills and when the farmer's neighbours sympathised with the old man over his bad luck, the farmer replied, "Bad luck? Good luck? Who knows?"

A week later, the horse returned with a herd of horses from the hills and this time the neighbours congratulated the farmer on his good luck. His reply was, "Good luck? Bad luck? Who knows?"

Then, when the farmer's son was attempting to tame one of the wild horses, he fell off its back and broke his leg. Everyone thought this very bad luck. Not the farmer, whose only reaction was, "Bad luck? Good luck? Who knows?"

Some weeks later, the army marched into the village and conscripted every able-bodied youth they found there. When they saw the farmer's son with his broken leg, they let him off.

Now was that good luck or bad luck? Who knows?

Everything that seems on the surface to be bad may be a good thing in disguise. And everything that seems good on the surface may really be bad.

So we must bear all the circumstances that life brings with equanimity and resilience and with an attitude that 'this too shall pass'.

. . .

Source: Unknown

Mental Toughness: Control & Challenge

My takeaways:

1. Life happens. Both the good and the bad. The question is, 'what is good and what is bad?' Invariably, it is the meaning we attach to the events, not the events themselves that make something good or bad.
2. Our mindset and our actions are the only two things we have true control over. Accept this and you'll be more resilient.
3. Mentally tough people focus on what they can control. They also look for the opportunity and learning in every event.

Questions:

1. What could you control that you are not presently controlling?
2. How could you think like a mentally tough person about a recent event that caused you some stress or upset? What can you learn from it?
3. How can you remember to look for the good in every 'bad' situation?

5

The Cricketer

In 1986, young Australian cricketer Dean Jones, was suffering from an acute case of dysentery and vomiting while playing in his first test for his country in India.

Jones was at the crease in 40-degree heat with oppressive humidity and 30,000 hostile Indian fans baying for his wicket.

Despite these challenging circumstances, the boy from Victoria scored a century. At the tea break in the afternoon, a fellow player, Steve Waugh, had to help him change out of his sweat-drenched whites and into a fresh set.

He went back out and by the time he had scored 120, he thought he was going to collapse from heat-stroke. Despite this he showed immense will and determination and went on to score another 30 runs, putting him on 150. At that point, he crumbled and told his batting partner and captain, that he could not go on.

His captain, Allan Border was furious and sarcastically replied, "Sure, mate, you go off and when you do ask them to send in a Queenslander because that's what we need out here."

Stung by this remark, Jones showed high-levels of mental toughness and stayed at the crease, going on to score a staggering 210 runs. This proved to be his highest ever score in test cricket.

It took him six months to fully recover physically from the effort and landed him in hospital for a while after the game.

. . .

Primary Source: Paul Lyons; Secondary Source: The Sydney Morning Herald

Mental Toughness Factors: Emotional Control, Life Control, Commitment, Confidence In Abilities, Challenge

My takeaways:

1. The mind will often quit long before the body does. By staying at the crease, Jones showed high levels of mental toughness to push his body past what he thought it was capable of.
2. When we can find a motivation that's strong enough we can often exceed what we initially think we are capable of.
3. Sometimes we can have too much mental toughness. Was it really worth putting his health at risk for a game of cricket? That's not for us to judge. We each have to decide

what price we are willing to pay to achieve our goals, but be aware that too much mental toughness can be a bad thing sometimes.

Questions to consider:

1. What would you have done in that situation?
2. If he had chosen to quit despite the sarcastic remark from his captain, would that have shown any less mental toughness?
3. Has there been a time when you have pushed through despite wanting to quit? How did you feel afterwards?

6

A Story of Courage

In April of 1940, Christian the Tenth, the King of Denmark, gazed out of a palace window.

The city had recently fallen to the advancing German army as it swept across Europe faster than the Coronavirus.

As he did, he saw the Swastika flying above Government buildings.

The King immediately insisted on a meeting with the Commander of the German forces and politely asked that the flag be taken down. This request was denied.

Pondering this refusal for a moment, he replied, "And what if I send a soldier to remove it? What will you do?", he asked?

"Quite simply, I will have him shot on the spot," said the Commander abruptly.

"I don't think so," replied the King, "not when you see who I will send."

"Please explain," said the Commander, "I am intrigued as to who we should fear."

The King straightened his back and looked the commander squarely in the eye, and with a calm and steady voice, replied, "I will be that soldier."

The story has it that the flag was removed within the hour.

. . .

Source: Mette Theilgard

Mental Toughness Factors: Emotional Control, Confidence in Abilities, Interpersonal Confidence

My takeaways:

1. At all the times the King was in control of his emotions. This allowed him to think more clearly and rationally. This is a hallmark of the mentally strong.
2. Our fears are often worse than the reality. When we stand up to bullies they often back down.

Questions to consider:

1. When have you lost your emotional control recently and how would maintaining it have served you better?
2. In what situations is someone trying to bully you in to

something you don't want to do?

3. What if you acted like the King and calmly explained why you won't do what they ask? What would that do for your confidence? What's the worst that can happen?

7

Roger Bannister

On Thursday, 6th May 1954, a young medical student changed the mindset of the world in under four minutes. Three minutes, fifty-nine and four-tenths of a second, to be precise.

At the Iffley Road running track in Oxford, watched by 3,000 people, Roger Bannister became the first man in history to run a mile in under four minutes. Until that historic moment, the perceived wisdom from so-called experts was that it was not possible for a man to run so fast.

"The idea that this sub-four-minute mile was impossible was, in my view, a myth. Whether we as athletes like it or not, the four-minute mile had become rather like an Everest - a challenge to the human spirit," he said.

Bannister's story is not one of continued success. Only two years before, he was widely expected to win gold at the Helsinki Olympics, yet he failed, trailing home in fourth place. At the time Bannister was developing his own training methods and his failure at the Olympics drew much criticism. "I felt it was necessary to prove my attitude towards training had been right and hence restore the faith that had been so shaken by my Olympic defeat," he wrote his in autobiography.

Despite the criticism and the punishing schedule of studying medicine full time, Bannister set himself the goal of running the mile in under four minutes. "I felt that in my running I was defending a cause...if my attitude was right then it should be possible to achieve great success and I wanted to see this happen - both for myself and for friends."

On the chosen day, Bannister doubted the weather conditions justified an attempt as the wind was fierce. At 11am he went into the hospital and sharpened his spikes on a grindstone in the lab. 'You don't think that's going to make a difference do you?" someone asked him. Unperturbed, he rubbed graphite on the spikes so that the wet cinder of the track would not stick as much to them.

As he travelled to the track Bannister had almost decided to postpone the attempt. His coach said, "Roger, the weather is terrible but even as bad as it is, I think you are capable of running under four minutes. Who knows when or if you may get another chance. If you pass it up today, you may never forgive yourself for the rest of your life."

With half an hour to go, Bannister was still undecided and then in a moment, he decided to change his mindset. "Right, we'll go for it, we all know what we have to do," he told his running partners.

With only 50 yards to go Bannister was spent, "My body was exhausted but went on running all the same. The physical overdraft came only from greater will-power," he said.

. . .

Source: Twin Tracks, Roger Bannister

Mental Toughness Factors: Contol, Commitment, Challenge, Confidence

My takeaways:

1. One man's mindset as to what was possible, coupled with his mental toughness to make it happen, changed the mindset of the world.
2. Bannister's story is a great reminder that there are only two things we have any control over in life: our mindset and our actions.
3. Look what can be achieved when we focus on those two things.

Questions to consider:

1. How well are you controlling your mindset and actions?
2. What would you do if you knew you could not fail?
3. What are you waiting for?

8

The Lesson of The Archer

Attaching too much importance to external outcomes distracts you from the important internal ones.

Consider the archer. If he is shooting for the joy of shooting, he will be relaxed and with an easy focus. Using all his skills and experience.

If he is shooting to qualify for the Olympics he may become tense and begin to doubt himself.

If the prize is Olympic gold in a shoot-off with another archer, he may become weighed down with expectation and the fear of losing.

In all three scenarios, the archer's skill is the same but in the last two he has fallen into the thinking trap of magnification and the importance of material rewards. He loses sight of who he is.

When we put too much attention and focus, especially on 'losing' things we don't yet have, we become clumsy and perform badly.

To avoid this, know what is important in your life and know what is unimportant.

. . .

Source: Taoist tradition

Mental Toughness: Control, Confidence, Challenge

My takeaways:

1. When we do things for the love of doing them we don't feel stress or pressure.
2. We often fear losing something we don't have. You can't lose a game or a client, because you haven't yet won them.

Questions:

- What is really important in your life?
- What is actually unimportant that you currently think is important?
- Have you ever performed without fear or stress?
- When you did, what was the difference in your mindset?
- How much better did you perform?

9

God & The Farmer

One day a priest was driving across the country to take a position in a new parish in a farming community.

As he was nearing his destination, he came over the brow of a hill, he saw a beautiful view down in the valley. In the centre of the valley lay one of the prettiest farms he had ever seen. Bright red farm buildings stood grandly at the centre of freshly ploughed fields, which were bordered by sturdy white fencing.

The farmhouse was well maintained and framed by hanging baskets of brightly coloured flowers. Attracted by the moving sight, the priest decided to introduce himself to the farmer. As he slowly drove down the lane to the house the farmer appeared on his tractor at the side of a field he was sowing with a new crop of wheat.

With a cheery wave, the farmer stopped his machine and nonchalantly stepped down and ambled his way over the priest, who had got out of his car.

"Hello," said the priest, "I must say this is one of the prettiest farms I've ever seen."

The farmer, a man in his late 50s with a friendly but a weather-worn face from years of hard toil turned to admire the view. "Thank you, Father," he said, that's most kind of you."

"God has truly blessed you with with a stunning part of the world, said the priest.

"Hmm," said the farmer smiling ruefully, "it is indeed a beautiful farm, but you should have seen it when God had it all to himself."

. . .

Source: Bob Proctor

Mental Toughness Factors: Control & Commitment

My takeaways:

1. We have the raw ingredients to do amazing things, what matters is whether we choose to put the work in.
2. Your mind is like the farmer's field. It will grow weeds or it will grow crops, the difference is what you choose to plant and how well you tend to it.
3. Nothing worthwhile comes easily.
4. Other people rarely appreciate the effort it takes to achieve great things.

Questions to consider:

1. What are you planting in your mind, weeds or crops?
2. How well are you tending to your mind?
3. What's one thing you could improve your likelihood of success?
4. Are you guilty of giving up too soon before you have achieved your goals?

10

The Hole

One evening, a man walking home after a night out, thought he saw a fifty-pound note at the bottom of a deep hole in roadworks near the city centre.

He jumped in to grab it but was disappointed. It wasn't a fifty-pound note. It was a food wrapper.

Then he realised the fifteen foot sheer walls made it impossible to get out of the hole.

He called for help, but no-one came. The city fell dark and silent.

He got cold and frightened. He couldn't see a way out and he didn't know what to do.

Then when he thought all was lost, he heard a voice from above. It shouted:

"Are you OK?"

"No, I'm stuck. I can't get out" he shouted back.

"How come?"

"The walls are sheer; I can't climb them."

"OK, hang on. I'll help you."

With that, the man jumped into the hole.

The first man berated him:

"Why have you jumped in here? Now we're both stuck."

"No," said the second man, "I've been in this hole before and I know how to get out."

. . .

Source: Peter Whent

Mental Toughness Factors: Emotional Control, Challenge, Confidence

My takeaways:

1. The first man acted emotionally to the prospect of free money. If he had paused for a moment he would have likely seen the risks in the situation and chosen to act differently.

Learning to manage our emotions to both the good and bad in life can pay dividends.

2. The second man had learnt from his first experience of being in the hole and demonstrated confidence in his abilities. He had learned from his past adversity. Don't avoid adversity but look to what you can learn from it. What skills can you develop?

Questions to consider:

1. What situations or people cause you to react emotionally and too quickly?
2. How can you practice stepping back before reacting?
3. When have you learned from adversity?
4. What strengths and qualities did you use during that time?
5. How have you grown?

11

The Old Crocodile

The old crocodile was floating at the river's edge when a younger crocodile swam up next to him,

> *"I've heard from many that you're the fiercest hunter in all of the river bottoms. Please, teach me your ways."*

Awoken from a nice long afternoon nap, the old crocodile glanced at the young crocodile with one of his reptilian eyes, said nothing and then fell back asleep atop the water.

Feeling frustrated and disrespected, the young crocodile swam off upriver to chase after some catfish, leaving behind a flurry of bubbles. *"I'll show him"*, he thought to himself.

Later that day the young crocodile returned to the old crocodile who was still napping and began to brag to him about his successful hunt,

> *"I caught two meaty catfish today. What have you caught?*

Nothing? Perhaps you're not so fierce after all."

Unphased the old crocodile again looked at the young crocodile, said nothing, closed his eyes and continued to float atop the water as tiny minnows munched away lightly at the algae on his underbelly.

Again, the young crocodile was angry he couldn't get a response from the elder, and he swam off a second time upstream to see what he could hunt.

After a few hours of thrashing about he was able to hunt down a small crane. Smiling, he kept the bird in his jaws and swam back to the old crocodile, adamant about showing him who the true hunter was.

As the young crocodile rounded the bend, he saw the elder crocodile still floating in the same spot near the river's edge.

However, something had changed — a large wildebeest was enjoying an afternoon drink just inches near the old crocodile's head.

In one lightning-fast movement, the old crocodile bolted out of the water, wrapped his jaws around the great wildebeest and pulled him under the river.

Awestruck the young crocodile swam up with the tiny bird hanging from his mouth and watched as the old crocodile enjoyed his 500 lb meal.

The young crocodile asked him, *"Please... tell me... how... how did you do that?"*

Through mouthfuls of wildebeest, the old crocodile finally responded,

"I did nothing."

. . .

Source: Aytekin Tank

Mental Toughness Factors: Emotional Control, Life Control, Confidence In Abilities, Interpersonal Confidence

My takeaways:

1. The old crocodile was confident enough in his abilities that he didn't need to prove himself to the younger croc.
2. The young croc was lacking in emotional control to wait. His impulsiveness to act meant he wasted lots of energy for little reward.
3. The younger croc also lacked confidence in his abilities and tried to mask it with boasts and bravado.

Questions to consider:

1. In what areas of your life and dealings are you being impulsive and lacking emotional control?
2. What are you trying to prove and to whom?

3. What if you slowed down and focused your energy on fewer things? What might you catch?

12

The Tale of Two Seeds

Late one summer, two seeds found themselves side by side in a furrow of a ploughed field.

Shortly after the farmer covered them over with soil to protect them from the foraging birds and coming winter.

Huddled together they remained there throughout the winter. They were aware of the days getting shorter and the colder weather as the warm autumn rains changed into the cold winter snows. They were glad they were protected by the warm blanket of the soil as the snow grew thicker above them.

Patiently they waited.

Winter began to turn into spring and as it did so, they both began to feel strange feelings stirring inside themselves.

One of them began to wonder if the snows had gone and what lay above her, so she began to push up little green shoots through the soil. At the same time, she wondered what lay beneath her, so she pushed out roots in all directions to see what she could find.

The other seed was too timid though. "I've no idea what might be out there," he said. "I'm safe and warm in here so I think I'll just stay right here, a little bit longer."

As the days went by the first seed grew stronger as the rays of spring sunshine fed her little shoots and water and nutrients in the soil fed her growing roots. All the while, the other seed did nothing, too scared to venture out of its comfort zone, stifled by the little voice inside his head that told him it might be dangerous.

By early summer the first seed stood tall and proud. Standing several feet above the ground she could see far and wide and felt great pride in having grown so tall and strong. The other seed remained with its risk-free strategy.

Until a big magpie came along and ate it.

. . .

Source: Russian fable

Mental Toughness Factors: Challenge & Confidence

My takeaways:

1. To live is to risk - if we risk nothing, we gain nothing.

2. Mental toughness is not about an absence of fear or risk but about acting in spite of these.
3. True confidence comes from being willing to risk failure in order to grow. When we grow and learn from success and failures then we develop confidence.

Questions to consider:

1. In what areas of your life are you behaving like the second seed?
2. When have you taken a risk and how did that pay-off for you?
3. How do you currently see failure - as something to avoid or learn from?

13

The Miracle on The Hudson

On 15 January, 2009, US Airways Flight 1549 took off from La Guardia airport in New York for a flight to Charlotte, North Carolina.

At the controls was pilot Captain Chesley Sullenberger. Shortly after take-off and with the plane at only 2,800ft a flock of birds struck the plane, instantly stopping both engines. With no power and 155 people on board including himself, Capt. Sullenberger had to quickly evaluate the situation and decide on the correct course of action.

With time ticking away and precious altitude dropping while still over New York, he chose to land the plane on the Hudson River. This despite the fact that two other airports were close by and the traffic controller was telling him he could make it.

Every single person survived the water landing and only a few suffered minor injuries. Despite the immense pressure and the tiny window of time in which to make the right decision,

Capt Sullenberger was able to maintain his composure and land successfully.

He was also able to maintain his composure when, during the formal investigation, it was suggested he could have made it to a nearby airport and saved the plane. Despite the intense scrutiny and seemingly overwhelming evidence to the contrary, he was able to think more clearly and rationally and highlight the fundamental flaw in the enquiry's findings.

Once he did this, they themselves proved he could not have reached an airport and he indeed did make the correct decision.

. . .

Source: Highest Duty, by Chesley Sullenberger. Published by Harper Collins

Mental Toughness Factors: Emotional Control, Life Control, Confidence In Abilities, Interpersonal Confidence

My takeaways:

1. What made the difference was Capt. Sullenberger's emotional and life control. His ability to manage his emotions allowed him to think clearly and evaluate the situation from several angles. He focused on what he could control.
2. This was supported by his confidence in his ability to land the plane on the river, something he had never done before.
3. Emotional control and the ability to extend the gap

between event and response also helped him when it came to the investigation. He saw what others missed.

Questions to consider:

1. In what areas of your life and dealings are you being impulsive and lacking emotional control?
2. What could you do to extend the gap between the event and your response?
3. How can you develop higher levels of confidence in your abilities?
4. How often when presented with a surprising or challenging set of circumstances do you focus on the things you can control rather than worry about the thing itself?

14

The Old Man & The Kids

An old man moved into a council house on the edge of a large estate. Soon some of the local kids started to gather around his house and make a nuisance of themselves. They'd throw litter in his garden and shout insults at him at all times of the day.

After a few days of this, the old man came out of his house and spoke to the kids. "Is that the best you can do?" said the old man. "Where I came from the kids could shout much louder than you and they were better at coming up with insults. They were far more inventive than you. I tell you what," he said, "come back tomorrow and if you can do better I'll give you one pound each."

"You're on old man," said the leader of the kids, "we'll be back tomorrow." They went home that night and looked up all sorts of nasty insults and swear words and came back the next day.

"Not bad at all," said the old man the next day, "but I bet you can do better than that surely. I tell you what, come back tomorrow even better and louder than today and I'll give you each 50p pence."

The next day, like clockwork, the kids returned, this time with even more choice and colourful language and at a louder level. After an hour of this, the old man once more came out to talk to them.

"Well done, he said, you've surpassed yourselves. Can you do better tomorrow, I wonder? Come back and show me, but this time I can only afford to pay you, ten pence each."

"What," they exclaimed, "only ten pence? That's not worth the effort."

They didn't come back the next day or any day after that. It wasn't worth it.

. . .

Source: Adapted from More Magic of Metaphor, by Nick Owen

Mental Toughness Factors: Emotional Control & Life Control

My takeaways:

1. By maintaining his emotional control in the face of bad behaviour the old man retained the upper hand.
2. He showed high levels of life control and focused on what he could control and influence and let go of the rest.
3. The creativity of thought and understanding of what

motivates people is often better than direct confrontation.

Questions to consider:

1. Who are the 'children' in your life?
2. How have you been reacting so far?
3. How could you respond to challenging behaviours as the old man did?

15

The Fox & the Hedgehog

Most of us would probably agree, that when it comes to the fox and the hedgehog, the fox is smarter. The fox is quick and cunning, creative and persistent, finding many ways to outwit and capture its prey. It's also adaptable to the traps that humans lay and finds ways to evade capture. In some respects, it could be said he bears many of the hallmarks of mental toughness.

The hedgehog, however, although capable of a surprising burst of speed is less gifted. It looks like a cross between a toilet brush and a tiny ant-eater. It spends its days foraging for food and looking after its nest. Lower to the ground and with a soft underbelly, the hedgehog feels every bump on the ground. He might represent someone who is more mentally sensitive.

Despite these disadvantages, the hedgehog often outsmarts the fox. The wily fox lies in wait for his bumbling prey and when he sees it, he moves with stealth, speed and precision. Surely, he makes an easy meal of the hedgehog. He doesn't though, with a minimum amount of effort, the hedgehog rolls into a ball and sharp spines protect him from the fox.

Despite all his qualities and attributes, the fox goes home hungry. It can be the same with mental toughness. Sure, having a high level of mental toughness can help. It can mean that we are better able to deal with the stress, pressures and challenges of life but it does not guarantee success.

Equally, mentally sensitive people, while they may feel every bump in the road, can still be successful. There are many qualities that come with mental sensitivity, such as empathy, a warmness, creativity. Mentally sensitive people can be nice to be around.

What matters most to both types of people is their level of self-awareness. The more self-aware, the more each person can choose the response that will serve them best in any given situation. The mentally strong person can moderate if required, some of their natural strengths. The mentally sensitive person can choose to act in a way that a mentally strong person might, should the situation call for it.

Source: Aesop's Fables and other sources

Mental Toughness Factors: Control, Commitment, Challenge, Confidence

My takeaways:

1. What matters as much as mental toughness is emotional intelligence and self-awareness.

2. Mental sensitivity is not mental weakness.
3. The world needs foxes and hedgehogs. Every team needs a balance of people, of personality types and degrees of mental toughness.

Questions to consider:

1. Are you naturally more fox or hedgehog?
2. What are your strengths and weaknesses?
3. How can you develop more self-awareness?

16

The Water Boy

Once upon a time, a young Sri Lankan boy had to make the daily trek to get water for his family.

Each day he would set off with a large pole across his shoulders and two large pots, one at each end. He would make the one mile round trip to the nearest well, where he would fill up both empty pots and walk back with them.

One day he dropped one of the pots and cracked it. Over the course of his walk back, some of the water would leak out. By the time the boy reached his house about half of the water had been lost from the pot. To hide this from his mother he would quickly decant both pots into a large pot.

One day, after weeks of this, his mother noticed the crack when he returned and the fact that half of the water was missing. She told him off for not fixing it and for trying to hide it from her.

"Why didn't you think to get it fixed," she said crossly. "You have been wasting your effort by only coming back with three-quarters of the water you could have."

The boy apologised and ran off. A short while later, he returned and handed his mother a beautiful bunch of flowers to say sorry. "Where did you get these beautiful flowers," she asked? "We don't have money to buy these."

"These are from the side of the path I take when I walk back with water," he said. "The water from the cracked pot falls on the dry earth and helps these flowers grow. I noticed this and that's why I didn't get the crack repaired as I thought it would give us fresh flowers we could sell."

His proud mother beamed at him, "What a clever boy you are and thank you for my lovely flowers. I will keep these and we will sell the others."

. . .

Source: Adapted from Sri Lanka

Mental Toughness Factors: Commitment & Challenge

My takeaways:

1. In life, we will all experience failure. What matters though is how to interpret that failure.
2. The mentally strong person looks to see what can be learnt from the failure and is also open to new ideas and opportunities that may come from it.

Questions to consider:

1. How do you react to a failure that you have had? Did you only look at the bad in the situation or did you look for learning and opportunity?
2. How do you respond when others fail? Do you berate them as the boy's mother did at first or do you pause before responding and ask a different set of questions such as: What did you learn from this? What could you try differently next time? What good might come from this?
3. In the face of failure are you as kind to yourself and others as you might be?

17

The Girl and The Duckling

The doctor looked at the young girl's eyes and knew there was little that could be done for her now. Her cancer was not responding to treatment and so he decided to send her back home to the care of her family.

Three months later he was astounded, and even more delighted, when she walked back into his clinic, her eyes bright and pain-free. She wore a healthy glow and energy he had never seen her possess. Without having to run more tests he knew she was in remission and would likely live a long life.

Elated and equally dumbfounded, he spent a good deal of time talking to the girl about the last few months and what had made the difference. As they talked he learned, among other things, that on her way home from her last visit they came across an injured duckling at the side of the road.

The girl and her parents rescued the duckling and for the next three months, she slowly nursed it back to health and watched it grow. Only the day before her latest visit to the doctor, they had released it into the wild and watched it soar off into the distance to begin its new life.

"Aha!" said the doctor. "I've seen this before, a man, or a girl in your case, who has a 'why' can put up with almost any 'how'. When we care for something bigger outside of ourselves, it can often help us achieve amazing things."

. . .

Source: Adapted from Zen tradition

Mental Toughness Factors: Control & Commitment

My takeaways:

1. Random acts of kindness have been shown to boost mental toughness and our immune system.
2. As Viktor Frankl found, hope and purpose are essential factors in being resilient and caring for something or someone other than ourselves can lead people to often do extraordinary things.
3. The mind is often an underutilised tool in the fight against physical and mental illness.

Questions to consider:

1. When was the last time you carried out a random act of kindness and how did it make you feel?

2. What thing, person, or cause bigger than yourself could you focus on that would give you a sense of purpose?
3. Are you allowing the power of your mind to work for or against you?

18

The Black Dot

One day a teacher entered the classroom and asked his students to prepare for a surprise test. They waited anxiously at their desks for the test to begin. The teacher handed out the question paper with the text facing down as usual. Once he handed them all out, he asked his students to turn the page and begin. To everyone's surprise, there were no questions, just a black dot in the centre of the page.

The teacher seeing the expression on everyone's face, told them the following, "I want you to write about what you see there." The confused students got started on the inexplicable task. At the end of the class, the teacher took all the answer papers and started reading each one of them aloud in front of all the students. All of them with no exceptions described the black dot, trying to explain its position in the middle of the sheet etc.

After all had been read, the classroom was silent. The teacher began to explain, "I am not going to grade on you this, I just wanted to give you something to think about. No one wrote about the white part of the paper. Everyone focused on the black dot and the same happens in our lives. We have a white paper to observe and enjoy, but we always focus on the dark spots. Our life is a gift given to us, our friends around us, the job that provides our livelihood, the miracles we see every day."

"However, we insist on focusing only on the dark spots, the health issues that bother us, the lack of money, the complicated relationship with a family member, the disappointment with a friends etc. The dark spots are very small compared to everything we have in our lives, but they are the ones that pollute our minds. Take your eyes away from the black spots in your life. Enjoy each one of your blessings, each moment that life gives you. Be happy and live life positively!"

. . .

Source: Common metaphor

Mental Toughness Factors: Control

My takeaways:

1. There are only two things that we can control in our lives: our mindset and what we do.
2. The mentally strong person focuses on what they control only. By doing this they can influence other things. They let go of things they have no control or influence over.

Questions to consider:

1. What are you focusing on? The things you can control or things you can't?
2. What if you stopped focusing on the black dot in your life?
3. When was the last time you wrote down all the good things you have in your life?

19

The Invisible Lid

In an experiment, a scientist placed a number of fleas in a glass jar.

They quickly jumped out. He then put the fleas back into the jar and placed a glass lid over the top. The fleas began jumping and hitting the glass lid, falling back down into the jar.

After a while, the fleas, conditioned to the presence of the glass lid, began jumping slightly below the glass lid so as not to hit it. The scientist then removed the glass lid as it was no longer needed to keep the fleas in the jar.

Despite this, the fleas didn't jump out. They had developed the belief that this was as high as they could jump. They stopped trying.

. . .

Source: Common metaphor

Mental Toughness Factors: Control, Commitment, Challenge, Confidence in Abilities

My takeaways:

1. In life, we will all come up against invisible lids.
2. The mentally strong person persists longer than the rest and isn't afraid of the setbacks they may face. They know that sometimes the blocks to our progress may have been removed without our knowledge and so it's always worth persisting.
3. Often the biggest barriers to our achievements lie inside our heads, in the form of the stories we tell ourselves about who we are and what we are capable of.

Questions to consider:

1. What are your invisible lids?
2. What stories are you telling yourself about what you are capable of?
3. Where did these stories come from?
4. What if you tried one more time?

20

Are you a Carrot, an Egg or Coffee Bean?

Once upon a time, a daughter complained to her father that her life was miserable and that she didn't know how she was going to make it. She was tired of fighting and struggling all the time. It seemed just as one problem was solved, another one soon followed. Her father, a chef, took her to the kitchen. He filled three pots with water and placed each on a high fire.

Once the three pots began to boil, he placed carrots in one pot, eggs in the second pot and ground coffee beans in the third pot. He then let them sit and boil, without saying a word to his daughter. The daughter moaned and impatiently waited, wondering what he was doing. After twenty minutes he turned off the burners. He took the carrots out of the pot and placed them in a bowl. He pulled the eggs out and placed them in a bowl. He then ladled the coffee out and placed it in a cup.

Turning to her, he asked. "Daughter, what do you see?" "Carrots, eggs and coffee," she hastily replied.

"Look closer", he said, "and touch the carrots." She did and noted that they were soft.

He then asked her to take an egg and break it. After pulling off the shell, she observed the hard-boiled egg.

Finally, he asked her to sip the coffee. Its rich aroma brought a smile to her face.

"Father, what does this mean?" she asked.

He then explained that the carrots, the eggs and coffee beans had each faced the same adversity-the boiling water. However, each one reacted differently. The carrots went in strong, hard and unrelenting, but in boiling water, they became soft and weak. The egg was fragile, with the thin outer shell protecting its liquid interior until it was put in the boiling water. Then the inside of the egg became hard. However, the ground coffee beans were unique. After they were exposed to the boiling water, they changed the water and created something new.

"Which one are you?" he asked his daughter. "When adversity knocks on your door, how do you respond? Are you a carrot, an egg, or a coffee bean?"

Source: Various sources

Mental Toughness Factors: Control, Commitment, Challenge, Confidence

My takeaways:

1. In life, lots of things happen. Some are good, some are bad. Some are of our own making and some happen to us. What matters is not what happens as much as it is our response to what happens.

2. Mental toughness is about how we choose our responses. We all have a choice, each and every time. Sometimes, the right choice may be to yield, like the carrot, sometimes it might be to harden like the egg, sometimes it might be to change the situation like the coffee. To decide which is best we need to be clear about what our goal is. Always keep the end goal in mind.

3. "It's not what happens to you, but how you react that matters," - Epictetus.

4. It might not be your fault that something has gone wrong, but it is your responsibility to learn from it and to use it to move you forwards.

Questions to consider:

1. When have you been the carrot, the egg or the coffee? Did it help you achieve your end goal?

2. Which of the three do you tend to be like most often and does this serve you well?

3. How could you change, for the better, the way you think about one thing that's bothering you right now?

21

The Peacock & The Crow

A crow lived in the forest and was absolutely satisfied in life. But one day he saw a swan. "This swan is so pink," he thought, "and I am so black. This swan must be the happiest bird in the world."

He expressed his thoughts to the swan. "Actually," the swan replied, "I was feeling that I was the happiest bird around until I saw a parrot, which has two colours. I now think the parrot is the happiest bird in creation." The crow then approached the parrot. The parrot explained, "I lived a very happy life until I saw a peacock. I have only two colours, but the peacock has multiple colours."

The crow then visited a peacock in the zoo and saw that hundreds of people had gathered to see him. After the people had left, the crow approached the peacock. "Dear peacock," the crow said, "you are so beautiful. Every day thousands of people come to see you. When people see me, they immediately shoo me away. I think you are the happiest bird on the planet."

The peacock replied, "I always thought that I was the most beautiful and happy bird on the planet. But because of my beauty, I am entrapped in this zoo. I have examined the zoo very carefully, and I have realised that the crow is the only bird not kept in a cage. So for the past few days, I have been thinking that if I were a crow, I could happily roam everywhere."

. . .

Source: moralstories.org

Mental Toughness Factors: Confidence

My takeaways:

1. Nothing saps our confidence more than comparing ourselves to others. I call it 'comparisonitis'; the feelings of inadequacy that come from comparing ourselves to others and the trap that it creates for us.
2. True confidence comes from mastery; from getting better at something. We would be better off comparing ourselves against the person we were yesterday and no-one else.
3. We each have strengths and weaknesses compared to others. Spend more time developing your strengths and you'll develop the confidence to be the best version of you.
4. Confidence and happiness are often a matter of perception. The only perception that matters, is yours.

Questions to consider:

1. What are your strengths? What makes you, you?
2. Are you suffering from 'comparisonitis'?
3. What if you focused on developing your strengths even further, rather than looking at someone else? What would that do for your confidence?
4. What attributes and qualities do you have that make you, uniquely you?

22

Conclusion

So, there you are, twenty stories and metaphors about mental toughness. Which was your favourite? Which one resonated most with you?

What about your children? Which one did they like the most? I'd love to know your answers to these questions and any other feedback you might have for me. Please feel free to email me on anthony@threefifty9.com and I'll be sure to reply.

For me, there are three that impacted on me the most. I've chosen one for me as a person, one for my role as a parent and one for my career.

For me as a person, I think I've spent too much time and energy comparing myself to others and not appreciating my own strengths and qualities. That's why the last story of the peacock and the crow struck a chord with me.

As a parent, it would be the carrot, egg and coffee. Parenting is hard and it calls for a sometimes confusing blend of knowing when to soften, when to be hard and when to change the situation. I've got this wrong many times and it's a daily work in progress. I'm not perfect, I just hope I can do a good enough job that my children grow up to be happy, self-sufficient and resilient.

Lastly, career-wise, for too long I was like the young crocodile, impatient to learn fast and be successful. I didn't learn the quality of patience and that success takes time. I spent too much time being in a such a hurry and thrashing around chasing one goal after another it's amazing I achieved anything.

What would have helped would have been clear on my values and purpose. That's something I think the King of Denmark had. He knew what his values were and he knew what his purpose was and that was something that was bigger than himself. It was his country and to lead his people. When we are clear about our reason 'why' then we can put up with almost any 'how'. That helps us be mentally tough.

I hope you found something in each and every story and hope you that you just enjoyed the time and space to read them and reflect. We lead such hectic lives that it can be hard to switch off, and take even a few minutes for ourselves to be still and reflective.

Before you go, if you enjoyed this book, please give it a review on Amazon and share why you liked it. That will help others find the book and maybe get as much from it as you did. Now, would't that be cool?

Best wishes,

Anthony

. . .

References & Further Reading

If this has piqued your interest and you'd like to find out more about mental toughness and how this might be able to help you or your team, then do get in touch.

In the meantime you can learn by about mental toughness and metaphors from the following books:

Developing Mental Toughness, Peter Clough & Doug Strucharczyk, Kogan Page

Developing Mental Toughness in Young People, Peter Clough & Doug Strucharczyk, Routledge

The Magic of Metaphor: 77 Stories for Teachers, Trainers and Therapists, Nick Owen, Crown House Publishing

More Magic of Metaphor: Stories for Leaders, Influencers, Motivators, Nick Owen, Crown House Publishing

The Salmon of Knowledge: Stories for Work, Life, the Dark Shadow & OneSelf, Crown House Publishing

The Obstacle is the Way: The ancient art of turning adversity into opportunity: Ryan Holiday, Profile Books

The Daily Stoic: 366 Meditations on Wisdom, Perseverance, and the Art of Living: Featuring new translations of Seneca, Epictetus, and Marcus Aurelius by Ryan Holiday, Profile Books

Ego is the Enemy: The Fight to Master Our Greatest Opponent by Ryan Holiday

HBR's 10 Must Reads on Mental Toughness (with bonus interview "Post-Traumatic Growth and Building Resilience" with Martin Seligman) by Harvard Business Review

About the Author

Anthony runs ThreeFifty9, a mental skills speaking and training consultancy, that specialises in equipping people and teams with the mental skills needed to thrive in today's world. ThreeFifty9 focuses on developing personal and leadership performance through mental fitness - the application of mental toughness, emotional intelligence, and good mental health, combined.

Anthony brings the experience of a 20-year career across the private and public sector both nationally and internationally.

He held several Head of Communications positions in both public and private sector organisations and built a successful publishing company in the Caribbean.

Anthony has been coaching since 2006 and has chosen to work predominantly with middle managers as he believes they have the toughest job in business.

Over the last five years, Anthony has worked with clients across numerous sectors including social housing, professional services, automotive, public sector, armed forces, retail, construction, energy and technology. These include: KPMG, AO.com, Veolia, JLL, Royal Navy, Goldman Sachs and WH Smith to name a few.

You can contact with him at: anthony@threefifty9.com or via any of the methods below.

You can connect with me on:

- ⊕ https://www.threefifty9.com
- 𝕏 https://twitter.com/AntTaylor72
- 📘 https://www.facebook.com/Anthony-Taylor-10868408086003.
- ℰ https://www.linkedin.com/in/anthonytaylor-mentalfitness

Subscribe to my newsletter:

- ✉ https://sendfox.com/anthony

Also by Anthony Taylor

Anthony is an expert in mental fitness and personal development. He is currently working on two other books: The 60min Guide to Personal Resilience, and The Untroubled Mind. Sign up to his email list to receive updates and free chapters as these books progress.

He has also written a guide book to where he lived in the Caribbean, published by MacMillan.

Tips from the Top: The Secrets of How to Successfully Navigate Middle Management
This is a practical, easy to read collection of interviews with highly successful leaders who have successfully navigated middle management to reach the top. With refreshingly candid honesty about their mistakes as well as successes and absolutely no jargon or theories. Anthony interviews a wide range of men and women from around the world, from both the private and public sector as well as some acclaimed authors and leadership experts.

Turks & Caicos: Lands of Discovery (Macmillan)

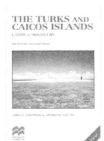

This 3rd edition of the ever popular guidebook has been fully updated to reflect the changes in visitor destinations from Grand Turk to Provo, while retaining the insight into the culture and history often overlooked in other guidebooks that combine TCI with The Bahamas.

.

Printed in Great Britain
by Amazon